THIS LAND CALLED AMERICA: **ARIZONA**

CREATIVE EDUCATION

Published by Creative Education
P.O. Box 227, Mankato, Minnesota 56002
Creative Education is an imprint of The Creative Company
www.thecreativecompany.us

Book and cover design by Blue Design (www.bluedes.com)
Art direction by Rita Marshall
Printed in the United States of America

Photographs by Alamy (Rick and Nora Bowers), Corbis (Tom Bean,
Bettmann, Dave G. Houser, George H. H. Huey, Charles O'Rear), Getty
Images (Dirk Anschutz, Tom Bean, John Blaustein, John Burcham,
Cameron Davidson, Carl Iwasaki/Time & Life Pictures, Donald Miralle,
Joe Munroe/Hulton Archive, Caroline Purser, Bert Sagara, Arthur
Schatz//Time Life Pictures, Time Life Pictures/National Archives/
Time Life Pictures, Diana Walker//Time Life Pictures, Randy Wells,
Frank Whitney)

Library of Congress Cataloging-in-Publication Data
Labairon, Cassandra Sharri.
Arizona / by Cassandra Labairon.
p. cm. — (This land called America)
Includes bibliographical references and index.
ISBN 978-1-58341-628-0
1. Arizona—Juvenile literature. I. Title. II. Series.
F811.3.L33 2008
979.1—dc22          2007015001

First Edition
9 8 7 6 5 4 3 2 1

*This Land Called America*

# ARIZONA

Cassandra Labairon

# Arizona

CASSANDRA LABAIRON

EVERY YEAR, NEARLY FIVE MILLION PEOPLE TRAVEL TO THE WESTERN UNITED STATES TO EXPLORE ARIZONA'S GRAND CANYON, THE LARGEST CANYON IN THE U.S. VISITORS STAND ON THE RIM OF THE GAPING CHASM, MESMERIZED BY THE VIEW OF THIS NATURAL WONDER OF THE WORLD. THEY TAKE PICTURES OR CONTEMPLATE THE VIEW. SOME HIKE DOWN INTO THE CANYON TO EXPERIENCE ITS MAGICAL LANDSCAPES AND RICH NATURAL HISTORY. ADVENTUROUS WHITE-WATER RAFTERS TAKE A WILD RIDE ON THE COLORADO RIVER RIGHT THROUGH THE HEART OF THE GRAND CANYON. SPRING, SUMMER, FALL, AND WINTER, THE STATE OF ARIZONA OFFERS ITS RESIDENTS AND VISITORS TASTES OF ADVENTURE AND BEAUTY.

YEAR
1540    Spanish explorer Francisco Coronado discovers the Grand Canyon.
EVENT

# Ancient Lands

CENTURIES BEFORE ITS STATEHOOD, ARIZONA WAS INHABITED BY MANY DIFFERENT TRIBES OF AMERICAN INDIANS. BETWEEN A.D. 700 AND 1300, PEOPLE SUCH AS THE ANASAZI LIVED IN THE MOUNTAINS AND FORESTS OF ARIZONA. THEY BUILT THEIR HOMES ON THE CLIFF FACES AND WERE KNOWN AS CLIFF DWELLERS.

*Hopi Indian girl*

More than 15,000 Hopi people (left), whose ancestors were the ancient Anasazi, continue to live in the dry lands of Arizona (opposite).

Other tribes lived in the deserts of Arizona. They built homes called pueblos and made irrigation systems that carried rainwater to their fields. They were known for their style of architecture, cloth, and pottery. People still live in the pueblos of Arizona. The Pima and Hopi tribes are descendants of early groups.

Between 1300 and 1500, Navajo and Apache tribes came to the area from Canada. Both groups were hunter-gatherers, and

YEAR

1821    Mexico gains military control of Arizona; U.S. trappers and traders first come into the area.

EVENT

- 7 -

they raided the villages of the other tribes. The
Apache in particular were fierce fighters.

Spanish explorers began coming to
Arizona in the 1530s. They believed that they
would find gold there. In 1540, one group, led
by Francisco Vásquez de Coronado, found the Grand Canyon.
In the mid-18th century, Spanish colonists began moving to
the area. Arizona stayed under Spanish rule until 1824, when
Mexico gained control. When the Mexican-American war
ended in 1848, Arizona again switched hands and became a
United States territory.

*Francisco Coronado
(above) tried to show
American Indians the
importance of becoming
Christians.*

When the U.S. took over, life changed for Arizona's native
tribes. Spain and Mexico had considered them citizens and
allowed them to own land. The U.S. government took away
their land, their homes, and their rights. Many then lost their
lives in the Indian Wars that followed.

Cochise was an Apache chief during the Indian Wars.
After fighting many battles, he finally negotiated a treaty for a
reservation in 1872. His tribe was allowed to remain in Arizona.
They stayed, but they were not treated well. A few years later,
another Apache chief, Geronimo, led his people against the
U.S. again in a fight for native rights. They surrendered in 1886
to General Nelson Miles in Skeleton Canyon, Arizona.

YEAR
1848    The U.S. takes control of most of Arizona after the Mexican War.
        EVENT

*Theodore Roosevelt Dam was named after the 26th president, who was in office while the dam was built.*

*Anasazi cliff dwellings*

Prospectors, or people looking for gold, began moving into the area in the mid-1800s. A few got lucky and found gold or silver, but most did not. In the 1870s, copper was discovered near the towns of Bisbee and Douglas. Copper mining remains one of Arizona's top industries today. Copper is used to make such things as wire, pipes, and computer chips.

In 1887, the Salt River flooded Phoenix, and the residents convinced the government to build the Theodore Roosevelt Dam to control the flooding and allow for irrigation of desert lands. This made farming possible and attracted new settlers to the area around Phoenix.

Arizona first applied to Congress to become a state in 1891, but its bid was rejected. It took Arizona more than 20 years to become a state. It was the last of the 48 contiguous (touching) states admitted into the union on February 14, 1912. Because it came into the union on February 14, Arizona is nicknamed the "Valentine State."

Since the 1940s, manufacturing and industry have replaced mining and farming as Arizona's primary sources of employment. In addition to manufacturing, tourism is a major industry in Arizona. People travel from all over the world to enjoy Arizona's dramatic landscapes and warm weather.

YEAR
**1862** Chief Cochise and the Apaches attack soldiers at Apache Pass, beginning a 10-year war.
EVENT

At Navajo National Monument, visitors can see how Arizona's early people built homes on the cliffs.

# Grand in Many Ways

ARIZONA IS PART OF THE "FOUR CORNERS" REGION. THE FOUR CORNERS IS THE ONLY PLACE IN THE U.S. WHERE THE CORNERS OF FOUR STATES TOUCH. ARIZONA'S NORTH-EASTERN CORNER MAKES CONTACT WITH ONE CORNER OF UTAH, COLORADO, AND NEW MEXICO. ON ITS WESTERN SIDE, ARIZONA BORDERS NEVADA AND CALIFORNIA. ITS SOUTHERN BORDER IS SHARED WITH MEXICO.

State bird: cactus wren

Arizona is perhaps most famous for the Grand Canyon. The Grand Canyon is one of the seven natural wonders of the world. The 1,217,403-acre (487,350 ha) Grand Canyon National Park is located in northwestern Arizona. It took thousands of years for the Colorado River to carve out the magnificent gorge. The widest point is 18 miles (29 km) across, and its deepest point plunges to 6,000 feet (1,829 m). Scientists, archeologists, and tourists study and explore the Grand Canyon.

Grand Canyon National Park was established in 1919. The area's national park status helps to protect the natural habitat of more than 1,500 rare plants and 500 animal species, including the endangered peregrine falcon. One of the reasons there is such a wide variety of life in the park is that there are five different climate zones, from forests of ponderosa pines on the canyon's rim to deserts below.

Two billion years of history can be seen in the canyon's layers of rock. The rock found at the top of the canyon was formed at least 250 million years ago. Below that are fossils from many different time periods. At the very bottom of the gorge is some of the oldest stone on Earth. This black stone is two billion years old.

*Arizona's state bird, the cactus wren (above), can be found in southwestern deserts such as those of Grand Canyon National Park (opposite).*

YEAR
1863    The Arizona Territory is created, with Prescott as its capital.
EVENT

T he 93,532-acre (41,422 ha) Painted Desert, or Petrified Forest National Park, is located in northeastern Arizona. Scientists believe that dinosaurs lived there more than 200 million years ago. The land at that time was tropical and forested. A great flood uprooted the trees, and sediment from the receding water covered the trees. It took thousands of years, but the fallen trees slowly turned to stone. The Petrified Forest National Park has the greatest number of fossilized trees in the world.

*Fossilized plants and dinosaurs (above) can be seen in the Petrified Forest, while Arizona's most famous national park offers views of the Grand Canyon (opposite).*

**1886**   Famous Apache chief Geronimo surrenders to the U.S. military at Skeleton Canyon, Arizona.

The native people first called Arizona *Arizonac* or *Arizume,* both words that mean "small spring." Water has played an integral part in Arizona's history. People living in the southwestern Arizona desert have had to learn how to bring water to their crops and homes.

Scientists believe that two billion years ago, Arizona was under a giant sea. The sea is long gone, and water shortages have been a problem in recent history. Arizona is a large, modern state with a great need for water. Eleven dams have been built in Arizona to help with irrigation, flood control, and hydroelectric power. The dams create artificial lakes. The largest dam is the Hoover Dam on the Colorado River, which made Lake Mead. This lake has an area of more than 230 square miles (596 sq km).

Arizona is a land of extremes. Some parts of Arizona receive almost 30 inches (76 cm) of rain a year, but the southwestern deserts get only 4 inches (10 cm). High in the mountains of central and northern Arizona, it can snow up to 100 inches (254 cm) during the winter months, while the average daytime temperature of most Arizona cities hovers around 70 °F (21 °C).

*Completed in 1936, the Hoover Dam is 726 feet (221 m) high and was named for President Herbert Hoover.*

*Many of the new housing developments that have been built in Arizona (opposite) are centered on recreational places such as golf courses.*

# Boom State

IN THE PAST 60 YEARS, ARIZONA HAS EXPERIENCED DRAMATIC GROWTH. THE POPULATION OF THE STATE HAS INCREASED MORE THAN 1,000 PERCENT DUE TO THE SUNNY WEATHER, PLENTIFUL OUTDOOR ACTIVITIES, AND GROWING BUSINESS OPPORTUNITIES. SOME THINK THAT THE DEVELOPMENT OF THE AIR CONDITIONER HELPED BRING PEOPLE TO ARIZONA, TOO, BECAUSE AIR

*One of Arizona's "five Cs" stands for cattle, and the state's many ranches are staffed by experienced cowboys and cowgirls (below and opposite).*

YEAR

1919    Grand Canyon National Park is founded by the U.S. National Park Service.

EVENT

- 20 -

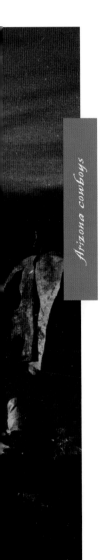

conditioning makes the hot summers bearable. Starting in April, many cities experience long streaks of days when the temperature registers 100 °F (38 °C) or higher.

Arizona residents proudly say their state is rich in the "five Cs." The five Cs include cattle, copper, cotton, citrus, and climate. Cattle and copper brought people to the area in the first part of the 20th century. Farmers came to the state when irrigation became possible. They tried growing a wide variety of crops. Today, Arizona's primary crop is lettuce, but Arizona farmers grow other vegetables as well as citrus fruits.

In the early 1900s, Arizona farmers started growing cotton. Cotton is used to make such things as clothing, paper products, and cottonseed oil. In recent years, manufacturing and industry have been attracted to Arizona. Large corporations have set up factories as well as corporate headquarters in the state. This new corporate and industrial boom has brought many new people to the state.

In the winter, many retired people from northern states spend time in Arizona. These people are known as "snowbirds." They live in Arizona for only part of the year. There are retirement communities in Arizona that offer opportunities for a variety of activities. The people living there can golf, swim, go for walks, and simply experience the grand Arizona landscape.

YEAR
1936    The Hoover Dam is completed on the Colorado River.
EVENT

Arizona has the third-highest number of American Indians in the U.S. Oraibi, a village on the Hopi reservation, has been continuously lived in for more than 800 years. That is longer than any other place in the U.S. The ancestors of non-native Arizona residents came primarily from Mexico, England, Ireland, and Germany.

Labor leader Cesar Chavez was born in Yuma in 1927 to a hardworking Mexican-American family. His family became migrant farm workers during the Great Depression and were treated poorly, paid little, and were constantly on the move. In the 1950s and 1960s, Chavez worked for a Latino civil rights group and cofounded the National Farm Workers Association. He organized strikes and nonviolent protests to help farm workers improve their working conditions.

*Sometimes farmers get creative when planting their crops and make them into shapes such as circles.*

*Cesar Chavez (opposite, center) was not formally recognized for his work until after his 1993 death.*

YEAR
1948 — The Arizona supreme court gives American Indians the right to vote in state elections.
EVENT

**A**rizona has been home to many amazing women. One woman who made great strides to help the people of Arizona was Annie Dodge Wauneka. Wauneka was the first woman elected to the Navajo tribal council in 1951. She was passionate about health care for the Navajo and fought for better health care on Arizona's reservations. She wrote a medical dictionary that translated English medical terms into the Navajo language. She also fought to stop the spread of diseases such as tuberculosis.

More recently, Supreme Court justice Sandra Day O'Connor helped influence many major decisions in America. O'Connor, who grew up on a ranch in southeastern Arizona, was appointed to the U.S. Supreme Court in 1981 and served for more than 25 years. In 2006, the year she retired, Arizona State University renamed its law school the Sandra Day O'Connor College of Law.

*Both Sandra Day O'Connor (above) and Annie Dodge Wauneka (opposite) spent their lives working on behalf of other people—in their state and throughout the country.*

1963 — Annie Dodge Wauneka is awarded the Presidential Medal of Freedom for her contributions to health care.

# Fun in the Sun

DURING ARIZONA WINTERS, PEOPLE CAN WATER SKI ON ONE OF THE STATE'S LAKES IN THE MORNING AND, LATER IN THE DAY, CAN SNOW SKI IN ONE OF THE STATE'S SKI AREAS. SUNRISE PARK RESORT, IN THE WHITE MOUNTAINS NEAR GREER, ARIZONA, BOASTS 65 SKI RUNS! IF AN EXPLORER WANTS MORE ADVENTURE, HE OR SHE CAN VISIT THE STATE'S NUMEROUS HISTORIC SITES

to learn about American Indians and Arizona legend. Each
site has a story.

One of the most famous stories of the Wild West happened in 1881 in Tombstone, Arizona. Gambling lawman Wyatt
Earp, his brothers, and gunfighter Doc Holliday had a deadly
showdown with a group of outlaws known as the Clanton
Gang at the OK Corral. Three members of the Clanton Gang
died, but the Earp brothers and Holliday survived. Visitors
to Arizona can see where the legendary shootout happened.

*Whether they're
taking in an Arizona
Diamondbacks baseball
game (opposite) or jet
skiing on a lake (above),
visitors can find
excitement.*

YEAR

| 1981 | Arizona justice Sandra Day O'Connor becomes the first woman on the U.S. Supreme Court. |

EVENT

*To point travelers in the right direction, colorful signs were placed along Route 66.*

To learn more about Arizona and its history, people can visit the Museum of Northern Arizona in Flagstaff. In 2007, the museum hosted its 74th annual Hopi Festival of Arts and Culture, which highlights traditional and modern forms of art by members of the Hopi tribe. Phoenix's Heard Museum and the Arizona State Museum exhibit both famous pieces of art and those that teach visitors about the state's history.

One of Arizona's treasures is U.S. Route 66. Four hundred miles (644 km) of historic Route 66 run through northern Arizona. The 2,448-mile (3,940 km) road was built in the 1920s to connect Chicago, Illinois, to Los Angeles, California. Small businesses soon opened along the route's roadside. Songs were written about its attractions, products were associated with its name, and the route was even glorified in books. In the late 1950s, states started to build large, four-lane highways. By the mid-1980s, Route 66 had been replaced by faster interstate highways. In the 1990s, groups in Arizona and a few other states brought parts of the road back so that travelers could relive part of American history. Arizona has the longest drivable stretch of the original Route 66.

Arizona is home to a number of professional sports teams. After only four years of playing in the National League, the Arizona Diamondbacks won baseball's World Series in 2001.

*Wigwam hotel*

YEAR
1991 | The Central Arizona Project uses a pipeline to transport water from the Colorado River to Tucson.
EVENT

- 28 -

*Route 66 offered many distinctive places to stay, such as these wigwam-shaped hotel rooms near Holbrook.*

## QUICK FACTS

Population: 6,166,318

Largest city: Phoenix (pop. 1,388,416)

Capital: Phoenix

Entered the union: February 14, 1912

Nickname: Grand Canyon State, Valentine State

State flower: saguaro cactus blossom

State bird: cactus wren

Size: 113,998 sq mi (295,253 sq km)—6th-biggest in U.S.

Major industries: mining, farming, tourism, manufacturing

Arizona's professional basketball team, the Phoenix Suns, has been a member of the National Basketball Association since 1968. In 1996, Arizona became the home of one of the first eight professional women's basketball teams, the Phoenix Mercury.

Although Arizona is known for its sun and heat, it is also home to an ice hockey team. The Coyotes are part of the National Hockey League, and they are coached by one of the most famous hockey players of all time, Wayne Gretzky. The Arizona Cardinals were one of the first members of the National Football League. Founded in 1898 in Chicago, the team is the oldest continuously run football team in America. The Cardinals play in Glendale, Arizona.

Arizona has been and continues to be one of the fastest-growing states in the U.S. Because much of the state is desert, the availability of water will play a major role in Arizona's future. With easier access to water, future generations will be able to continue enjoying the warmth and natural beauty of Arizona, the land of "small spring."

YEAR
2007 · NASA selects the University of Arizona as the first university to lead a mission to Mars.
EVENT

- 31 -

# BIBLIOGRAPHY

Ciovacco, Justine, Kathleen A. Feeley, and Kristen Behrens. *State-by-State Atlas*. New York: DK Publishing, 2003.

Gutman, Bill. *The Look-It-Up Book of the 50 States*. New York: Random House, 2002.

King, David C. *Children's Encyclopedia of American History*. New York: DK Publishing, 2003.

Mead, Robin, Polly Mead, and Andrew Gutelle. *Our National Parks*. New York: Smithmark, 1992.

National Park Service, U.S. Department of the Interior. "Experience Your America: Arizona." http://www.nps.gov/state/az/.

Young, Donald, and Cynthia Overbeck Bix. *Our National Parks*. San Francisco: Sierra Club Books, 1990.

# INDEX